Young Entrepreneurs

YOUNG ONES TO LEARN FINANCIAL LITERACY!!

AF791371

Tiya Peravali

UNSTOPPABLE SERIES -1

BlueRose ONE.com
Stories Matter
NewDelhi • London

BLUEROSE PUBLISHERS
India | U.K.

BlueRose ONE.com
Stories Matter
NewDelhi • London

For permissions requests or inquiries regarding this publication, please contact:

BLUEROSE PUBLISHERS
www.BlueRoseONE.com
info@bluerosepublishers.com
+91 8882 898 898
+4407342408967

ISBN: 978-93-7018-742-9

Cover Design: Aman Sharma
Typesetting: Pooja Sharma

First Edition: June 2025

Dedication:

To my amazing parents—

Thank you for believing in me, supporting my ideas, and always encouraging me to follow my dreams.

This book is for you, for all the love, time, and guidance you've given me every step of the way.

With all my heart,

Tiya Peravali

Acknowledgement:

I would like to thank my teachers and family for always encouraging me to learn and explore new things. Special thanks to my parents for supporting my love for reading, art, and financial literacy. This book is a result of everything I've learned and loved. I'm happy to share it with you!

— Tiya Peravali

Foreword:

In a world where financial awareness is vital, this book takes young minds on a fun and thoughtful journey through money, banking, business, and savings—with Priya as their curious guide. Through everyday questions and relatable stories, children can build a strong foundation in financial literacy that will grow with them.

Preface:

Dear Friends,

I am writing this book not only to explain the meaning of Finance but to encourage everybody to realise the power of Finance.

I wrote this book with the hope that children will be able to grasp the importance of the business world.

I really hope you like my series & one day start your own business.

Contents:

CREDIT CARD

1. Barter System:

In the old days, not everybody knew what currency or money was, so they couldn't buy things like we do now. Instead, they would trade commodities.

If Priya needed wheat & Arya needed rice, Priya had some rice & Arya had some wheat, they both would exchange the products which is called a Barter system.

DIGITAL RUPEE

2. Currency:

What is it? Why it is there? How its created?

Every type of money most likely got generated from the barter system. People wanted something equally valuable. So, all the governments created different forms of money, like in China they began with using swirled shells as money. Eventually people started creating metal coins.

And then few governments started using paper notes which is what we have even today.

Cryptocurrency:

A type of currency that is completely digital. It can be accessed through an account where you need to log in. Here you need to trade or buy different types of cryptocurrencies.

Some popular cryptocurrencies are Bitcoins, Ethereum, Tether, XRP, etc.

Latest Era – UPI is now being used everywhere instead of cash since its convenient - you barely need to scan, and the money is automatically transferred.

Priya was a curious kid, she wanted to know all about money, so she asked her mother about the types of money. And her mother told her that a few types of currencies are Indian rupees, US dollars, Euro/Liras etc.

3. Banking:

A bank is a safe place for one to keep their money. You can also take out money when needed for some purchase like a car, house or for personal use. The bank also pays you interest for keeping your money in the bank.

Bank can also lend you money if you need it. That's called a loan. Same way the bank charges interest in return.

Types of accounts - Demat, Savings, Current

Demat account – Is a specific account only meant for trading shares.

Savings account – Is an account where you can keep any amount of money & utilize it however you wish to for personal use.

Current account – Is an account that only the company who owns it can use , that too only for financial projects.

One day when Priya went to a shop and saw a complicated picture, she asked her mom what it was and she replied, "This is the code for transferring money to the shopkeeper".

4. Budget:

A budget is a financial plan relating to how you are going to spend your money. It's also about dividing money into needs & wants.

Priya always wanted to spend all her money on wants. Her father told Priya about budget. Soon, she made a chart about needs & wants. Then she divided her money. Now she could spend her money in an organized manner.

Goals

Item	Short-term or Long-term	Duration	Cost	Savings	Status

SAVE

5. Savings:

Savings is when one keeps some money aside for later use. This money is very important for emergency use, like medical issues.

One day, Priya saw her father savings some money in a safe. Priya had a habit of spending money all at once.

So, she asked her dad, "Why not spend everything at once?"

Her dad replied, "It's the power of savings. If we ever need emergency money, we can use this for personal use".

Now Priya understood the importance.

The best way of saving for children is Piggy Bank.

Needs vs Wants

Item	Needs	Wants	Cost	Savings	Achieved or not
Cycle	Yes		5.000	Started saving 1000 per month	Yet to
Phone		Yes	10,000	Not Required	Future Goal

6. Investment:

Investment is like planting a seed (money) and with enough care, getting a tree (more money). Now imagine that in the business world, you use money to get more money. Some investments one can do are, shares, real estate, mutual funds.

One day Priya heard her mother talking about investments.

"What is an investment?", she asked.

"Investments are when one invests money on something and it grows, until we get more money", said her mom.

When Priya grew up, she started investing her money in shares. With her knowledge, she even got a mutual fund & invested her money in it. This way as she grows up, her money also grows.

7. Trading:

Buying goods for low & selling for high to earn a profit is called trading.

Priya loved trading toys with her friends.

One day, when her dad was working, Priya asked him, "What is trading in business world?"

Dad said, "It's the same thing that you do, like mom buys stationary in bulk and sells it to all stationary shops in town for profit. As she sells more stationary, she gets more profit."

Priya now understood the importance of trading.

8. Insurance:

An insurance protects you financially if something bad happens like a damage or loss. You pay a small amount of money as premium to an insurance company, and in return they cover your asset.

Types of Insurances:

Auto Insurance – is only for vehicle damage like accidents

Life Insurance – would pay death bills if one passes away

Health Insurance – will pay for medical issues like hospital bills for surgeries

Priya had bought a new car. Since it was new, she thought it would be better to have a car (auto) insurance. Once day while driving she got into a very big accident. She was okay but it cost her 5 lakhs for her car. Since she paid 6 lakhs to the auto insurance, they paid the car repair company. It was then that Priya realized how important the insurance was.

9. Stock Market:

Stock can also be called share:

Stock is a small ownership of a company. It's like slices of pizza. When you buy stock, you are owning a small portion of ownership in the company.

Companies sell stock to raise money for their business.

Stock market is a place where people buy and sell shares of a company.

One can buy multiple stocks.

In India, we have National Stock Exchange (NSE) & Bombay Stock Exchange (BSE) for buying & selling shares.

Priya has purchased few shares in a food company. She had checked the financial status of the company. The company was performing well, so she was getting good profits.

One time Priya invested in a juice company. It was performing very poor, as the demand went down. Soon she got into a big loss.

10. How to Earn Money & How to Start Business:

There are 5 tips to help start business:

1. Get business idea
2. Take adult advice
3. Tell your ideas to potential customer
4. Write the idea
5. Find money to start business

One day while Priya was playing, she got an amazing idea to start a café. She told her parents about it and took their advice. Following the steps, Priya found a good place to start her cafe. Soon she got many customers and earned good returns.

About the Book:

This book introduces children to the world of money and finance through the curious mind of Priya, a young girl eager to learn. From the barter system to modern digital payments, Priya explores key concepts like savings, budgeting, investment, banking, insurance, trading, and the stock market in a simple, relatable way. With fun examples and real-life situations, children will understand how money works and how to manage it wisely. Whether it's starting a business or using a piggy bank, this book empowers young readers with essential financial literacy skills for a smarter, more confident future.